Dear, Sweet

Happy First Mother's Day!

Lisa

Beautiful
Flowers in
the Garden
of Life

A FIRESIDE BOOK

Published by Simon & Schuster
New York London Sydney Singapore

BABIES
ARE LIKE
BLOSSOMS

JANET LANESE

FIRESIDE

Rockefeller Center

1230 Avenue of the Americas

New York, NY 10020

Permissions Acknowledgments appear on page 128.

Designed by Barbara M. Bachman

Manufactured in the United States of America

1 3 5 7 9 10 8 6 4 2

Library of Congress Cataloging-in-Publication Data

Babies are like blossoms / [compiled] by Janet Lanese.

p. cm.

"A Fireside Book."

1. Infants — Quotations, maxims, etc. 2. Infants — Poetry. I. Lanese, Janet.

PN6231.I5 B33 2000

305.232 — dc21

99-050012

ISBN 0-684-86216-6

To Dani Flynn Budnieski, who dreamed of

motherhood for so long and then at forty delighted

us with beautiful twins, Chase and Dylan.

•

Kudos also to Dani's husband, Bob, the

"World's Greatest Father,"

who adores his two new tax deductions.

ACKNOWLEDGMENTS

Thanks to Laurie Harper of Sebastian Agency,

and Betsy Radin Herman, Marcela Landres,

and Matthew Walker of Fireside Books,

the most dynamic team in the publishing world!

CONTENTS

A LABOR OF LOVE

The family you come from isn't as important as
the family you're going to have.

Ring Lardner

Cravings: in which we discover that an insane desire for
a peanut butter, pickle, and Hershey Bar sandwich on
date nut bread is absolutely nothing to be alarmed about.

Peter Mayle

I like trying (to get pregnant). I'm not so sure about childbirth.

Lauren Holly

Familiarity breeds children.

Mark Twain

What is more thrilling than hearing your unborn child's
heartbeat for the first time?

Janet Lanese

There is no economy in going to bed early to
save electricity if the results be twins.

Chinese proverb

Babies are such a nice way to start people.

Don Herold

Have you ever noticed that most expectant mothers glow with a beautiful radiance?

Janet Lanese

What kind of a mother would rather be rich and thin than pregnant?

Erma Bombeck

Life does not begin with conception, but when the kids leave home, and the dog dies.

Russ James

Just think of pregnancy as having company inside your stomach.

Anonymous

THE POSITIVES OF PREGNANCY

The perfect excuse for a new wardrobe.

No more exhausting Jazzercise classes.

People offer a seat to you on public transportation (sometimes!).

You can have your favorite food without guilt.

An extended vacation from your outside job. Ha!

You suddenly have major cleavage.

You get to take catnaps throughout the day.

People put up with your sudden mood swings (maybe).

Your mate starts babying you (when he's in the mood).

Your friends and relatives give you baby showers where
you are gifted with delicious baby things.

Janet Lanese

Have children while your parents are still young enough
to take care of them.

Rita Rudner

How can a small child tell if his mother is pregnant?
His parents begin to spell things!

Janet Lanese

Childbirth:
The epidural was better than the sex that got me there.

Caryl Kristensen

I didn't know how babies were made until
I was pregnant with my fourth child.

Loretta Lynn

Making the decision to have a child — it's momentous.
It is to decide forever to have your heart go
walking around outside your body.

Elizabeth Stone

The greatest fantasy many pregnant women have during
that time when the imagination seems particularly ripe is that
of a fairy godmother called childcare.

Alice Kahn

My mother asked me what would I like best, a brother or a sister?
I told her to forget about a baby and buy me a puppy.

Jamie, age eight

I feel sure that unborn babies pick their parents.

Gloria Swanson

Sign on maternity clothes shop:
WE'RE OPEN LABOR DAY

Sign on hospital maternity ward door:
PUSH, PUSH, PUSH!

Anonymous

Most of the new mothers I know miss
being pregnant. That was the easy part.

Janet Lanese

Childbirth classes neglect to teach
one critical skill. How to breathe, count, and
swear all at the same time.

Linda Filterman

When the doctor asked me if I wanted
a bikini cut for my Cesarean section, I said,
"No! A bikini and a
wine cooler is why I'm lying here now."

Kim Tavares

HYSTERICAL PREGNANT PATIENT:
"Doctor, my water just broke! What should I do?"

DOCTOR:
"Well, you can start by getting off my new couch!"

Janet Lanese

YOUNG HUSBAND:
"Why don't you look like you did when we got married?"

DISGUSTED WIFE:
"Because I'm 8½ months pregnant, silly. That's why!"

Anonymous

Having a baby is like
trying to push a grand piano
through a transom.

Alice Roosevelt Longworth

The trouble with children is
that they're not returnable.

Quentin Crisp

When I was giving birth, the nurse asked,
"Still think blondes have more fun?"

Joan Rivers

Hard labor: A redundancy, like "working mother."

Joyce Armour

Childbirth is more admirable than conquest,
more amazing than self-defense,
and as courageous as either one.

Gloria Steinem

If Men Gave Birth . . .

They would demand twelve months' maternity leave with
    full pay and benefits.

All sexual activity would cease for the next nine months.

They would advocate marriage and monogamy.

Birth control classes would be mandatory in kindergarten.

Women would be shopping at 3 a.m. for ice cream and pickles.

A pill would be available to prevent multiple births.

Paternity suits would be designer business attire.

Natural childbirth would be replaced by laughing gas and mega-
    doses of morphine.

Briefcases would be plastic lined and come in pink and blue.

Nautilus would introduce gym equipment for postnatal workouts.

All babies would be bottle-fed.

Federally subsidized nannies would provide twenty-four-hour
    child care until the baby is potty-trained.

The first words out of every baby's mouth would be "Da da!"

Janet Lanese

If men had babies, maternity leave would be in the Bill of Rights.

Corky Sherwood Forrest

My mother had morning sickness after I was born.

Rodney Dangerfield

A babe at the breast is as much pleasure as the bearing is pain.

Marion Zimmer Bradley

I had a Jewish delivery: they knock you out with the first pain;
they wake you up when the hairdresser shows.

Joan Rivers

There is no privacy about a birth.

Margaret Mead

I'd be happy to stand next to any man I know in
one of those labor rooms the size of a Volkswagen truck
and whisper, "No, dear, you don't really need the Demerol,
just relax and do your second-stage breathing."

Anna Quindlen

My mother groan'd,
My father wept,
Into the dangerous world
I leapt.

William Blake

About the only thing we have left that actually discriminates
in favor o' the plain people is the stork.

Kin Hubbard

If newborns could remember and speak, they would emerge
from the womb carrying tales as wondrous as Homer's.

Newsweek

Always end the name of your child with a vowel,
so that when you yell, the name will carry.

Bill Cosby

Blessed are the young for they shall
inherit the national debt.

Herbert Hoover

When you want a child,
you have a lot to hope for.
When you have a child,
you have a lot to live for.

Jan Blaustone

NEW FATHER:

"The birth of a baby costs thousands!"

NURSE:

"Sure, but it's worth it. Look at how long they last!"

Anonymous

To my embarrassment I was born
in bed with a lady.

Wilson Mizner

There are two things in this life for which we are
never fully prepared, and that is twins.

Josh Billings

The birth of a child erases all previous marital agreements.

Susan Cheever

You can sort of be married, you can sort of be divorced, you can
sort of be living together, but you can't sort of have a baby.

David Shire

Being able to have the childbirth experience you want is powerful and meaningful. The feeling that you can achieve great things extends into all other aspects of your life.

Judith Zimmer

In creating a child, we invest all that we are in a future.

Paul Brenner

Have you noticed there are more
multiple births than ever before? Is it fertility drugs or,
with such an unsettled world,
are babies afraid to come out alone?

Janet Lanese

Yes, having a child is surely the most beautifully
irrational act that two people in love can commit.

Bill Cosby

We begin life with loss. We are cast from the womb
without an apartment, a charge plate, a job, or a car.

Judith Viorst

Birth is love made visible.

Paul Brenner

A baby is the little rivet in the
bonds of matrimony.

Anonymous

Of all the joys that lighten suffering
on earth, what joy is welcomed
like a newborn child?

Caroline Norton

You should study not only
that you become a mother when
your child is born, but also
that you become a child.

Dōgen

Every baby born comes with a link to the past,
and a promise for the future.

Janet Lanese

Life began waking up and loving my mother's face.

George Eliot

You were courted and got married in the magic world,
but you had your baby in the real one.

Bess Streeter Aldrich

For any normal woman in normal circumstances, there is
bound to be a special excitement and joy and gratitude
to God when she holds her first baby in her arms.

Rose Fitzgerald Kennedy

It sometimes happens even in the best families that a baby is born.
This is not necessarily cause for alarm. The important thing is to
keep your wits about you and borrow some money.

Elinor Goulding Smith

Newborn twins go through eighteen diapers a day.
Don't you feel better already?

Jan Blaustone

The birth of every new baby is God's vote
of confidence in the future of man.

Imogene Fey

My mommy told me the baby needs
to be treated tenderly. She's soft in the head.

Michael, age six

Here's a motto for all breast-feeding mothers — there's a little sucker
born every minute — thanks for the mammaries.

Dominic Cleary

We just happen to like children.

Frances Bless on the birth of her eighteenth child

When I was born, I was so surprised,
I couldn't talk for a year and a half.

Gracie Allen

Why don't babies come with step-by-step instructions?

Jeffrey, age eight

Twins: Womb-mates.

Kay Francis

In the sheltered simplicity of the first days
after a baby is born,
one sees again the magical closed circle.
The miraculous sense
of two people existing for each other.

Anne Morrow Lindbergh

Now the first thing about having a baby —
and I can't be the first person to
have noticed this — is that
thereafter you have it.

Jean Kerr

The moment you have children yourself,
you forgive your parents everything.

Susan Hill

My Baby

Baby . . . _My_ Baby
God gave you to me
You look like your Daddy
And a little like me

I carefully count
All your fingers and toes
Yes . . . I think
You have Grandma's nose

I have loved you
So very much
Even before
That very first touch

Even from
That very first kick
Even though
I felt . . . oh so sick

I loved you when
My belly was fat
I would rub it
And give you a pat

This love I feel
For you inside
Flows deep as a river
And just as wide

A love that's pure
Binding and true
A love that transcends
All . . . I once knew

Baby . . . _My_ baby
Now you are here
I'll always love you
So never fear

Your life has a plan
You're a part of mine too
Joys and sorrows
We'll both walk through

But when we are older
And live far apart
Baby . . . _My_ baby
You'll be . . . In my heart

For my daughter
Love, Mom
L. S. Alvarez 7/17/98

• 31

IT'S A GIRL!

Announcement from the proud parents of a baby daughter:
We have skirted the issue.

Earl Wilson

Your friendship with your daughter begins the
first time you hold her in your arms.

Marie Chapian

I've been trying to think of the last thing that awed me.
The only thing I can come up with is the birth of
my daughter almost five years ago.

Leonard Pitts, Jr.

I wonder if little Tammy can understand all those
adults who speak baby talk to her. I sure can't!

Susie, age seven

Loveliness beyond completeness,
Sweetness distancing all sweetness,
Beauty all that beauty may be —
That's May Bennett, that's my baby.

William Cox Bennett

A daughter is to her father a
treasure of sleeplessness.

Ben Silva

Of course I love my baby sister.
That's what she's here for, isn't it?

Diana, age five

Say the word "daughter," slowly,
prolong its gentle sound.
Notice the way it lingers on the tongue
like a piece of candy.

Paul Engle

It is hard to raise sons; and much harder to raise daughters.

Sholem Aleichem

Three daughters and people ask,
"Were you upset that the third child was a girl? " I say,
"No, not at all. I'm whittling a boy out of wood right now. "

Bob Saget

My friends ask is there a difference
between having a son or a daughter.
No doubt about it, the day my daughter was born
everyone began to look like a potential molester to me.
"Ho, ho, ho my ass — she's not sitting on your lap."

Jack Coen

A daughter is an embarrassing and
ticklish possession.

Menander

The hair she means to have is gold,
Her eyes are blue, she's twelve weeks old.

Frederick Locker-Lampson

Being a daughter is only half of the equation:
bearing one is the other.

Erica Jong

MOTHER:

"Do you know what happens to little girls who tell lies?"

DAUGHTER:

"Yes, they grow up and tell their little girls they'll get curly hair if they eat their spinach."

Anonymous

My baby sister probably will never learn to talk. Why should she? The little brat gets everything she wants by screaming.

Timothy, age seven

What Is a Little Girl?

A little girl is a charter member of the Junior League.

A little girl is a rosy-cheek innocent with stars in her eyes.

A little girl is her grandma's angel, her daddy's sweetheart,
and her mother's cherished baby.

A little girl is a wee pixie who crawls up on your knee
to give you a hug.

A little girl is a tease and nuisance to every boy under eighteen.

A little girl can be a dainty lady in ruffles and lace, or a
dirty-faced tomboy in jeans and sneakers.

A little girl is energy, imagination, curiosity, and a total delight.

A little girl can pout, stomp, and cry one moment and
act like a little princess the next.

A little girl is nature's first improvement on boys, and as
a woman is the last thing civilized by man.

A little girl uses the same universal language as boys, "gimme,"
translated as "I wanna."

A little girl is part of the world's most important generation,
a bank where you can deposit your most precious treasures.

Janet Lanese

The knowingness of little girls
Is hidden underneath their curls.

Phyllis McGinley

Of all the things that I would rather,
It is to be my daughter's father.

Ogden Nash

What are little girls made of?
Sugar and spice, and everything nice;
That's what little girls are made of.

Anonymous

When it comes to little girls, God, the father,
has nothing on father, the god.
It's an awesome responsibility.

Frank Piton

A tiny daughter gives parents a life in
a climate of perpetual wonder.

Pierre Doucet

Nursing a Toddler

Sticky little chubby hands pull my shirt;
  clearly it's time to nurse.
Now I have blue yogurt on my white bra;
  I know it could be worse!
She's too busy for cuddles and kisses;
  we nurse to keep us in touch.
She wants to be big like her big sister;
  sometimes it's just too much.
So up on Mama's lap she climbs again,
  For comfort and a snack.
I hold her close, sweet and soft as she rests,
  glad my baby is back.
I watch as she acts so independent,
  but nursing reminds me
Not to hurry her to grow up too fast,
  for time will still find me.
Friends try not to act surprised but all say,
  "When will she ever wean?"
I smile, "Well, I guess when she has classes
  She can nurse in between!"

Janis Chrissikos

Oh, high is the price of parenthood.
And daughters may cost you double.
You dare not forget, as you thought you could
That youth is a plague and trouble.

Phyllis McGinley

There was a little girl
Who had a little curl
Right in the middle of her forehead;
And when she was good
She was very, very good,
But when she was bad she was horrid.

Henry Wadsworth Longfellow

FRUSTRATED MOTHER:
"Now, Sally, be a good girl and say 'ahhh' so the doctor
can get his finger out of your mouth."

Anonymous

Sure little girls can act like angels—just as long as
anyone doesn't ruffle their feathers.

Josh, age twelve

Savana

soft little face
          fine blond hair
round blue eyes
          that seem to stare

abundant laughter
          sprinkled with tears
a trusting innocence
          untouched by fear

little hands
          so busy be
reach out for life's
          simplicity

with heart that's pure
          so meek and mild
a blessing sent
          is nature's child

                    Judy Meggers

IT'S A BOY!

From good parents
comes a good son.

Aristotle

Any mother with half a skull knows
that when Daddy's little boy becomes
Mommy's little boy,
the kid is so wet he's treading water!

Erma Bombeck

You don't raise heroes, you raise sons.
And if you treat them like sons, they'll turn out
to be heroes, even if it's just in your own eyes.

Walter Schirra, Sr.

Fathers, I think, are most apt to appreciate
the excellence and attainments of their daughters;
mothers, those of their sons.

Menander

Jody

Joodyy . . . Jooodyyy! . . . Joooodyyy! . . .

But Jody's not coming

He's not coming Jody

He has other plans

He has a new agenda Jody

He's going to Alaska

Where no one will find him

He took his sadness

Rolled it into a bundle

Threw it on his shoulder

And left

He left forever

He's gone forever

But when he comes back

Ten years later (Jody's time)

When he comes back

One-sixth of an hour later (our time)

Help with his bundle

Help him unfold it

Help him put it back in his drawer

Help Jody come home

When he comes back

Ten minutes later.

Andre S. Newton

Bouncing Baby Boy

A bouncing baby boy,
    wrapped up in clothes of blue.
With booties, gown, and knitted cap,
    for all the friends to view.

A mother dreams of great success,
    her perfect son to be.
Doctor, lawyer, president,
    what is his destiny?

In father's thoughts his son appears,
    a tall, athletic man
Football, golf, or tennis pro,
    with trophies in his hand.

But for the present, time stands still,
    and love turns into joy.
While happy hearts give thanks to God,
    for a healthy baby boy.

Judy Meggers

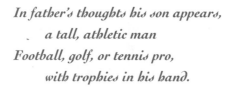

What Is a Little Boy?

A little boy is perpetual hunger with a milk mustache.

A little boy is a natural explorer who lives in the world of
imagination and feeling.

A little boy is a dirty-faced cherub, full of energy, noise,
and curiosity.

A little boy, with a twinkle in his eye, is a natural prankster,
and as unpredictable as an earthquake.

A little boy is drawn to any body of water, except the hot,
soapy kind.

A little boy is nature's rebuttal to the theory there is no such
thing as perpetual motion.

A little boy is a born chaser, running after fire engines, parades,
garbage trucks, other kids, or anything else that moves.

A little boy is a creature who is always halfway between his
mom or dad and mischief.

A little boy wears out three things: his sneakers, his favorite toys,
and his parents.

A little boy faithfully mimics his father despite his mother's
efforts to teach him good manners.

A little boy is the promise of tomorrow, the hope of a nation.

Janet Lanese

My sister just had a baby boy. I can't believe
I'm an aunt! It sounds so mature.

Kimberly, age twelve

The zest with which a boy does
an errand is equaled
only by the speed of a turtle.

Anonymous

If my baby brother is miserable,
the whole household is miserable.

Abby, age ten

One trouble in raising a boy is that father always
expects son to do exactly as much work
as he never did.

Anonymous

Still as my horizon grew,
Larger grew my riches too;
All the world I saw or knew
Seemed a complex Chinese toy,
Fashioned for a barefoot boy!

John Greenleaf Whittier

Mother had a little book
In which she wrote each day
About her little baby
And the cute things he would say.
She wrote about his first steps
And what he wanted to be
And if it's ever published,
He wants a royalty.

Martha Bolton

I remember when I first got my foster son.
He was the cutest little guy
I'd seen in my life. As I changed him,
I was surprised by how much I liked it.
I knew that I'd do what needed to be done.
But there was always that little voice
in the back of my head that said,
"Remember the saxophone was in the closet after a month."

Paula Poundstone

A fairly bright boy is far more intelligent
and far better company than the average adult.

J.B.S. Haldane

A boy, if not washed too often and if kept in a cool, quiet place
after each accident, will survive broken bones, hornets' nests,
swimming holes, fights, and nine helpings of pie.

Anonymous

Of all the wild animals, the boy is the most unmanageable.

Plato

Boyhood: A summer sun.

Edgar Allan Poe

One of the best things
in the world to be is a boy;
it requires no experience,
but needs some practice
to be a good one.

Charles Warner

MOTHER:
"Do you know what happens to
little boys who tell lies?"

SON:
"Yes, Mom, they get into
the amusement park for half price."

Anonymous

I am persuaded that
there is no affection
of the human heart more exquisitely pure,
than that which is felt by a
grateful son towards a mother.

Hannah Moore

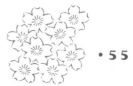

Don't wait to make
your son a great man—
make him a great boy.

Anonymous

Small boys are washable,
though most of them
shrink from it.

Times, *Fort Mill, South Carolina*

Boys do not
grow up gradually.
They move forward in spurts
like the hands of clocks
in railway stations.

Cyril Connolly

The only good thing
about my little brother's dirty diapers
is that they make him easy to find.

Laurie, age seven

When I was a boy,
I used to do
what my father wanted.
Now I have to do
what my boy wants.
My problem is:
When am I going to do
what I want?

Sam Levenson

Sons are the anchors
of a mother's life.

Sophocles

We think boys are rude, insensitive animals,
but it is not so in all cases.
Each boy has one or two sensitive spots, and if you
can find out where
they are located, you only
have to touch them and you can
scorch him as with fire.

Mark Twain

When we look at actual children,
no matter how they are raised,
we notice immediately that little girls
are in fact smaller versions
of real human beings,
whereas little boys
are Pod People from
the Planet Destructo.

Dave Barry

What are little boys made of?
Snips and snails, and puppy dogs' tails.
That's what little boys are made of.

Anonymous

The parent who could see
his boy as he really is,
would shake his head and say,
"Willie is no good, I'll sell him."

Stephen Butler Leacock

Nobody knows what a boy is worth,
    A boy at his work or play,
A boy who whistles around the place,
    Or laughs in an artless way,
Nobody knows what a boy is worth,
    And the world must wait and see,
For every man in an honored place,
    Is a boy that used to be.
Nobody knows what a boy is worth,
    A boy with his face aglow,
For hid in his heart there are secrets deep
    Not even the wisest know.
Nobody knows what a boy is worth,
    A boy with his bare, tan feet;
So have a smile and a kindly word,
    For every boy you meet.

Anonymous

• 59

IN THE WEE WEE HOURS OF THE MORNING

A baby is God's opinion that life should go on.

Carl Sandburg

I just can't get over how much babies cry.
I really had no idea what I was getting into.
To tell you the truth, I thought it would
be more like getting a cat.

Anne Lamott

Newborn infants are not always pretty to look at,
but they are always beautiful.

Janet Lanese

Man is of woman born, and her face bends
over him in infancy with an
expression he can never quite forget.

Margaret Fuller

Heaven lies about us in our infancy!

William Wordsworth

Although it is generally known, I think it's about time
to announce that I was born at a very early age.

Groucho Marx

Isn't it strange how many parents see a strong resemblance
between their baby and their wealthiest relative?

Janet Lanese

We haven't all had the good fortune to be ladies;
we haven't all been generals, or poets, or statesmen;
but when the toast works down to the babies,
we stand on common ground.

Mark Twain

It's dangerous to confuse children with angels.

David Fyfe

If I were a new baby, I don't think I could stand knowing
what I was going to have to go through. That's why they don't show
them any newspapers for the first two years.

Charles M. Schulz

When the cry of the newborn
enters your lodge,
consider it singing, and it will
not be so annoying.

Shaman Chief Kitpou

Babies are beautiful because they defy
all races, colors, and creeds.
They're all simply sweet,
innocent beings . . . and *everyone* loves a baby!

Dani Flynn Budnieski

There are lots of things that you can brush
under the carpet about yourself until you're faced
with somebody whose needs
won't be put off.

Angela Carter

People who say they sleep like a
baby usually don't have one.

Leo J. Burke

Our neighbor's baby has the best of everything.
In fact his stroller is fancier than our family car.

Jeffrey, age nine

Wee Babies

Babies short and babies tall,
Babies big and babies small,
Blue-eyed babies, babies fair,
Brown-eyed babies with lots of hair,
Babies so tiny they can't sit up,
Babies that drink from a silver cup,
Babies that coo and babies that creep,
Babies that only can eat and sleep,
Babies that laugh and babies that talk,
Babies quite big enough to walk,
Dimpled fingers and dimpled feet,
What in the world is half so sweet
As babies that jump, laugh, cry, and crawl,
Eat, sleep, talk, walk, creep, coo and all,
Wee babies?

Eugene Field

I like it when the babysitter comes. She's so busy trying
to keep the baby dry, fed, and asleep that
I can get away with murder!

Kim, age seven

I knew I was an unwanted baby when I saw
that my bath toys were a toaster and a radio.

Joan Rivers

I once knew a chap who had a system of just hanging the baby
on the clothes line to dry, and he was greatly admired
by his fellow citizens for having discovered
a wonderful innovation on changing a diaper.

Damon Runyon

Have you ever noticed that
the second baby isn't half as fragile as the first?

Janet Lanese

No animal is so inexhaustible as an excited infant.

Amy Leslie

VISITOR:

"Your baby really seems to love you."

FATHER:

"He certainly does! Why, he sleeps all day while
I'm working, and stays up all night just for
the pleasure of my company."

Janet Lanese

If you desire to drain to the dregs the fullest cup of scorn
and hatred that a fellow human being can pour out for you,
let a young mother hear you call dear baby "it."

Jerome K. Jerome

My point is that no matter what the ordinary person says . . . no
matter who it is that speaks, or what superlatives are employed,
no baby is admired sufficiently to please the mother.

E. V. Lucas

A child is helpless in inverse ratio to his age. He is at the zenith
of his powers while he is an infant in arms. What on earth
is more powerful than a very young baby?

Aline Kilmer

Babies are necessary to grown-ups. A new baby is
like the beginning of all things—wonder, hope,
a dream of possibilities.

Eda J. Le Shan

To have children is a double living, the earthly fountain of youth,
a continual fresh delight, a volcano as well as a fountain and
also a source of weariness beyond description.

Josephine W. Johnson

I've never told this to anyone before, but when I was a baby,
I was breast fed from falsies.

Woody Allen

Since people are going to be living longer and getting older,
they'll just have to learn how to be babies longer.

Andy Warhol

A baby is the world's longest suspense story; you have to
wait for a generation to see how it turns out.

Anonymous

The baby wakes up in the wee wee hours of the morning.

Robert Robbins

Babies are forget-me-nots from
the angels' heavenly meadows.

Janet Lanese

A baby is born with a need to be loved
and never outgrows it.

Frank A. Clark

Among the three or four million cradles now rocking
in the land are some which this nation would preserve for ages as
sacred things, if we could know which ones they are.

Mark Twain

There is no finer investment for any community
than putting milk into babies.

Winston Churchill

A babe in a house is a well-spring of pleasure,
a messenger of peace and love,
a resting place for innocence on earth,
a link between angels and men.

Martin F. Tupper

I love children—especially
when they cry, for
then someone takes them away.

Nancy Milford

Adam and Eve had many advantages,
but the principal one was that
they escaped teething.

Mark Twain

Truly there is nothing
in the world so blessed or so sweet as
the heritage of children.

Carolina Oliphant

Now I know why my parents
tell me to be careful
and hold the baby's head.
It's the safest part.

Roger, age eleven

The infant's instinctive smile seems to have
exactly that purpose which is its crowning effect, namely,
that the adult feels recognized, and in return
expresses recognition in the form of loving and providing.

Erik Erikson

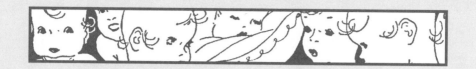

Moments to Remember

Juice stains on the carpet, Cheerios on the floor;
Toys scattered all over, handprints on the door.
Wet kisses on the cheek, showing that they care;
Strained peas on little hands, and peaches in their hair.
Kleenex strewn all over, CDs off the rack;
Grimy little hands, reaching for a snack.
Screaming very loud, when it's time to sleep;
Big wet tears staining their faces, whenever they may weep.
Little accidents in the tub, when they take a bath;
Cute little grins, that always make you laugh.
These moments won't last forever, better enjoy them while they last.
Mothers take heed my warning, they grow up much too fast!

Amy Mayberry

New Mothers

New mothers give up corporate offices for home nurseries.

New mothers give up "dressing for success" for "dressing for comfort."

New mothers give up pricey professional styling for a blow-dry à la naturelle.

New mothers give up dancing in the wee hours for walking the floor in the wee hours.

New mothers give up rock for lullabies.

New mothers give up the theater for a VCR.

New mothers give up Chardonnay for French roast.

New mothers give up gourmet cuisine for microwave dinners.

New mothers give up sixty-minute bubble baths for sixty-second showers.

New mothers give up Danielle Steel for Benjamin Spock.

New mothers give up workouts at the gym, long phone calls, fastidious housekeeping, and practically anything else for precious moments with their babies.

Janet Lanese

HUSBAND:

"It must be time to get up, dear!"

WIFE:

"How do you know?"

HUSBAND:

"The baby's fallen asleep."

Anonymous

What a Baby Costs

"How much do babies cost?" said he
the other night upon his knee;
And then I said, "They cost a lot;
A lot of walking by a cot,
A lot of sleepless hours and care,
A lot of fear and trying dread,
And sometimes many, many tears are shed
In payment for our babies small,
But every one is worth it all."

Edgar Guest

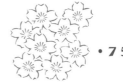

THE LAND OF LULLABIES AND SWEET DREAMS

Lullaby o lullaby!
Thus I heard a father cry,
Lullaby o lullaby!
The brat will never shut an eye;
Hither comes, some power divine!
Close his lids or open mine.

Thomas Hood

**Families with babies and families
without babies are sorry for each other.**

E. W. Howe

**Have you ever met a
baby who couldn't
upstage an adult?
Me neither.**

Janet Lanese

A Baby Is . . .

The next generation:
A tiny human with unlimited power —
A bundle of joy, and oh so lovable.
Soft little hands grasping your fingers.
Baby powder mixed with sour formula.
Dancing eyes following a fluttering mobile.
Today's investment, tomorrow's dividend.
The most perfect of God's creations.

Janet Lanese

In every child who is born, under no matter
what circumstances, and of no matter what parents,
the potentiality of the human race is born again;
and in him too, once more, and each of us,
our terrific responsibility towards human life;
towards the utmost idea of goodness,
of the horror of error; and of God.

James Agee

Nothing could or ever would
be too good for your baby.

Janet Lanese

Don't forget that compared to a grown-up person,
every baby is a genius. Think of the capacity to learn!
The freshness, the temperament, the will
of a baby a few months old.

May Sarton

*A bit of talcum
Is always walcum.*

Ogden Nash

Beginnings

A baby to hold and to love,
a creature so tiny, so fresh and so new.
There's nothing more important or special
That two loving people could ever do.
Who will the baby look like?
Will it be a he or she?
Part of him, part of her,
a creation that is meant to be.
All we could ever want for our baby
is very simple and very plain
It's to be happy and content in life
and know our love will never wane.

Nicol Campise

**Mother's milk is the thing for babies. It's nutritious,
cheap, satisfying, and doesn't make crumbs.**

Milton Berle

By the way, many people make the
false assumption that because a baby can't speak,
he can't hear. As a result, when confronted
with an infant, any infant, they raise their
voices and speak very distinctly, as though
they were ordering a meal in
a foreign language.

Jean Kerr

Babies are bits of stardust,
blown from the hand of God.
Lucky is the woman
who knows the pangs of birth,
for she has held a star.

Larry Barretto

Babies have it made!
Who else gets to sleep twenty hours a day?

Jessica, age fifteen

The law of grab is the
primal law of infancy.

Antoinette Brown Blackwell

Anyone who uses the phrase "easy as taking candy
from a baby" has never tried taking candy from a baby.

Anonymous

While admitting that adults frequently
make unfortunate remarks to babies,
it has to be said that babies, too,
can make mistakes.

Jean Kerr

A child, like any creation or work of art,
changes all that precedes it.

Paul Brenner

When the first baby laughed for the first time, the laugh broke
into a thousand pieces and they all went skipping about,
and that was the beginning of fairies.

James Matthew Barrie

A baby is an inestimable
blessing and bother.

Mark Twain

I'm sure glad I'm not a baby anymore
like my sister Susanna.
She gets bathed at least twice a day,
and has to put up with as many
as six changes of clothes.
What's the harm of leaving her
a little dirty? She doesn't
go anyplace important.

Jonathan, age nine

Here we have a baby.
It is composed of a bald head
and a pair of lungs.

Eugene Field

Little children are still the symbol of
the eternal marriage between love and duty.

George Eliot

In point of fact, we are all born rude.
No infant ever appeared yet with
the grace to understand how
inconsiderate it is
to disturb others
in the middle of the night.

Judith Martin

STEPPIN' OUT
WITH MY BABY

Babies, like angels,
take themselves lightly,
and sprout wings
flying towards
independence.

Janet Lanese

It's all over now;
It's the day of doom.
He climbed out of the crib
And ran out of his room.

Maureen Wright

If only we could know
what was going
on in a baby's mind
while observing him in action,
we could certainly understand
everything there is
to psychology.

Jean Piaget

Life's too short . . .

to play enough pat-a-cake with your baby.

to think your kids will never be out of the diaper stage.

to know the interior of your office better than your child's face.

to complain about your kids while others long for a child.

to spend more time filling in the baby book

    than playing with the baby.

to forget the magic of the tooth fairy.

to realize how quickly children grow up . . . until they do.

Judy Gordon Morrow

Kids, they're not easy, but there has to be some penalty for sex.

Bill Maber

Most things have an escape clause . . . but children are forever.

Lewis Grizzard

I think that saving a little child
And bringing him to his own
Is a derned sight better business
Than loafing around the throne.

John Hay

When the children
were infants,
we didn't want them to grow up.
They were so dependent,
innocent, and cute.
If they had become
toilet trained
and swore off crying,
we would have kept them
just that way.

William Coleman

What are so mysterious as
the eyes of a child?

Phyllis Bottome

Correct infant care
is vital to producing
"Super Babies."
Super Babies are similar to
regular babies except
they belong to you.

P. J. O'Rourke

Babies don't want to
hear about babies;
they like to be told of
giants and castles.

Samuel Johnson

Never give your
one-year-old baby sister a
bowl of cereal and milk and
expect her to feed herself.
It's a real mess!

Ted, age nine

Always be nice to your children, because they are
the ones who will choose your rest home.

Phyllis Diller

Reasoning with a two-year-old is
about as productive
as changing seats
on the *Titanic.*

Robert Scotellaro

A child's education
should begin at least
one hundred years before
he is born.

Oliver Wendell Holmes

The only ones in our house
who never yell at me for
my dumb mistakes
are my dog and
my baby brother.

Jess, age seven

A One-Year-Old's Mind

Step on cereal
to hear it crunch.
Dump some orange juice
on my lunch.
I wonder what my
dog would do
If I gave him
Daddy's shoe?
Splash some socks
in the toilet bowl.
Drop a cup
and watch it roll.

Taste some dog food;
mmm, not bad.
Pull out tissues
one by one
Bang some pots —
this is fun!
I wonder what
my mom would do
If I colored
the sofa blue?
Hey, look! My mom
is jumping there,
And she's pulling
out her hair.

Maureen Wright

*A Christmas tree
with ornaments stripped,
Toilet Paper
unrolled and ripped.
Cans knocked down
in grocery stores,
Childproof locks
on every door.
Everything finished
becomes undone
Say no more—
your child is one.*

Maureen Wright

You know that the beginning is
the most important part of any work,
especially in the case of a young and
tender thing; for that is the best time at
which the character is being formed.

Plato

If a growing object is both fresh
and spoiled at the same time,
chances are it is a child.

Morris Goldfischer

I think my one-year-old brother is spoiled,
but my mommy tells me
all babies smell that way.

Trish, age five

For years we have given scientific attention
to the care and rearing of
plants and animals, but
we have allowed babies
to be raised chiefly by tradition.

Edith Belle Lowry

Grown men can learn from
very little children
for the hearts of little children are pure.
Therefore, the Great Spirit may
show to them many things which
older people miss.

Black Elk

Babysitter:
A person you pay who
invites friends to your house
to keep your children awake.

Anonymous

If you're a laughing parent,
your children will be laughing siblings,
who marry laughing spouses,
who give birth to
laughing grandchildren.
It's worth the investment.

Liz Curtis Higgs

102·

Warning to All Babysitters!

Always wear old clothes and
an oversized apron
when you watch small children.
The ones under six months
spit up their formula,
and those over six months
spit out their spinach.

Cindy, age sixteen

The best babysitters, of course,
are the baby's grandparents.
You feel completely
comfortable entrusting your baby
to them for long periods.
Which is why most
grandparents flee to
Florida at the
earliest opportunity.

Dave Barry

Before I got married,
I had six theories about
bringing up children; now,
I have six children and no theories.

John Wilmont

A torn jacket is soon mended;
but hard words bruise the heart of a child.

Henry Wadsworth Longfellow

There are only two things a child
will share willingly —
communicable diseases and his mother's age.

Benjamin Spock

When you've seen a nude infant doing a
backward somersault,
you know why clothing exists.

Stephen Fray

Children are born
motivated, not bored.
They come out into the world eager,
reaching, looking, touching—
and that's what
we want them to
keep on doing.

Dorothy Rich

It's clear that most
American children
suffer too much mother and
too little father.

Gloria Steinem

Parents of teens and parents
of babies have
something in common.
They spend a great deal of time
trying to get their kids to talk.

Paul Swets

In his youth, everyone believes that
the world began to
exist only when he was born,
and that everything really
exists only for his sake.

Johann Wolfgang von Goethe

The most cherished difference
between a baby and a toddler:
A baby receives hugs and kisses
A toddler can give them back.

Martha Bolton

IN PRAISE OF
PARENTHOOD

You Are Ready for Motherhood When:

You compliment your girlfriends on their maternity outfits.

Names for boys and girls keep popping into your head.

In bookstores you keep wandering into the Family section.

You collect stuffed animals and put them into your hope chest.

You forget to refill your birth control pill prescription.

You send for a subscription to *American Baby* magazine.

You put your mother's rocking chair in your bedroom.

You feel more amorous toward your husband.

You check out the best obstetricians.

You keep hugging and kissing your Golden Retriever.

Janet Lanese

You Are Ready for Fatherhood When:

You ask relatives and friends if you can hold their babies.

You buy a rocking horse for your den.

You trade in your sports car for a mini-van.

You forget to renew your NBA season tickets.

You sell your townhouse in the city for a split-level

    in the suburbs.

You double your life insurance coverage.

You install safety latches on the lower kitchen and

    bathroom cabinets.

You stop going out with the boys for a beer every Friday night.

You study *Consumer Reports* for the safest cribs

    and baby strollers.

You install a swing set in the yard.

Janet Lanese

The rules for parents are but three . . .
Love, Limit, and Let them be.

Elaine M. Ward

For our part we never understood the fear of some parents
about getting babies mixed up in the hospital.
What difference does it make so long as you get a good one?

Heywood Broun

Every mother practices the ritual of counting tiny fingers and toes,
cupping the small head in one's hand, stroking gossamer hair, and
trying to determine just whose side of the family is responsible for
these ears and that nose — these are rites of new motherhood,
both private and public, that mark the beginning of a new world.

Pamela Scurry

Father: A kin you love to touch.

Anonymous

You will always be your children's favorite toy.

Vicki Lansky

The job of a parent is to eventually do himself out of a job.

Alice Freedman

Raising children is a creative endeavor,
an art rather than a science.

Bruno Bettelheim

Friends who have recently discovered the joys of fatherhood lapse
into an utterly self-absorbed world. They exclude any childless dad
with the good sense not to be enamored by the dubious delights
of changing soiled diapers and other such pleasures
that may come with raising infants.

Albert Lubrano

Parentage is a very important profession, but no test of fitness
for it is ever imposed in the interest of the children.

George Bernard Shaw

Three stages in a parent's life: nutrition,
dentition, and tuition.

Marcelene Cox

A food is not necessarily essential just because your child hates it.

Katherine Whitehouse

Do not videotape your child in the bathtub.
Do not name your child after a Scandinavian deity
or any aspect of the weather.

Daniel Menaker

My mother taught me my ABCs. From my father
I learned the glories of going to the bathroom outside.

Lewis Grizzard

When one becomes a father, then first one becomes a son.
Standing by the crib of one's own baby, with that world-old pang
of compassion and protectiveness toward this so little creature
that has all its course to run, the heart flies back in yearning and
gratitude to those who felt just so toward one's self.
Then for the first time one understands the homely succession
of sacrifices and pains by which life is transmitted and fostered
down the stumbling generation of men.

Christopher Morley

Last night my child was born—a very strong boy, with large black eyes. . . . If you ever become a father, I think the strangest and strongest sensation of your life will be hearing for the first time the thin cry of your own child. For a moment you have the strange feeling of being double; but there is something more, quite impossible to analyze—perhaps the echo in a man's heart of all the sensations felt by all the fathers and mothers of his race at a similar instant in the past. It is a very tender, but also a very ghostly, feeling.

Lafcadio Hearn

The pressures of being a parent are equal to any pressure on earth. To be a conscious parent, and really look to that little being's mental and physical health, is a responsibility which most of us, including me, avoid most of the time because it's too hard.

John Lennon

Parents are often so busy with the physical rearing of children that they miss the glory of parenthood, just as the grandeur of the trees is lost when raking the leaves.

Marcelene Cox

116 •

Family life is too intimate to be preserved by the spirit of justice.
It can be sustained by a spirit of love which goes beyond justice.

Reinhold Niebuhr

Babies don't need fathers, but mothers do. Someone
who is taking care of a baby needs to be taken care of.

Amy Heckerling

Children are curious and are risk takers.
They have lots of courage, they venture out into
a world that is immense and dangerous. A child initially
trusts life and the processes of life.

John Bradshaw

*Oh, what a tangled web do parents weave
When they think that their children are naïve.*

Ogden Nash

Love is a parent's most powerful tool — and gift —
for raising happy, loving, and well-adjusted children.

Benjamin Spock

Truth, which is important to a scholar,
has got to be concrete. And there is nothing more
concrete than dealing with babies, burps
and bottles, frogs and mud.

Jeane J. Kirkpatrick

If you were going to wake up tomorrow as an infant,
would you choose to be raised by a daycare center, nanny,
or babysitter rather than parents? Don't do to your children
what you wouldn't choose for yourself.

Laura Schlessinger

Every baby needs a lap.

Henry Robin

Being a parent used to be one of the most simple,
natural, inevitable developments in the world.
But, nowadays, one has no business to marry unless,
walking and sleeping,
one is conscious of the responsibility.

Dr. Abraham Flexner

We never know the love of a parent till we
become parents ourselves.

Henry Ward Beecher

A family is a unit composed not only of children
but of men, women, an occasional animal,
and the common cold.

Ogden Nash

To a child's ear, "mother" is magic in any language.

Arlene Benedict

Another thing that Daddy ain't,
I frankly tell you, is a saint.

Ogden Nash

Spock, shlock, don't talk to me about that stuff.
A man doesn't know how to bring up children
until he's been a mother.

Dan Greenburg

Life is richer when one gives it to another.

Anonymous

Dads don't need to be tall and
broad-shouldered and clever.
Love makes them so.

Pam Brown

120·

The chances are that you will never be elected president of the country, write the great American novel, make a million dollars, stop pollution, end racial conflict, or save the world. However valid it may be to work at any of these goals, there is another one of higher priority—to be an effective parent.

Landrum R. Bolling

It's too bad that the most important job we have in life—parenting—is the one we have no training for.

Nancy Reagan

Parents are Patterns.

Thomas Fuller

Having family responsibilities and concerns just has to make you a more understanding person.

Sandra Day O'Connor

Half the fun of fatherhood is getting there.

Milton Berle

In automobile terms,
the child supplies the power but
the parents have to do the steering.

Benjamin Spock

I found the first few months of motherhood exhausting.
Of course, well-meaning souls who observed my bloodshot
eyes and down-turned mouth told me two things.

"Enjoy this time." — Give me a break.
What's so enjoyable about infants who stay up
all night, cry nonstop, constantly demand food,
and have erratic mood swings?
"It will never be like this again." — Hogwash.
When kids become teenagers, they do the
very same things, only louder.

Liz Curtis Higgs

Love begins by taking care of the closest ones —
the ones at home.

Mother Teresa

Everyone tells me that I've become much
mellower since I became a father.

Burt Reynolds

Children spell "love" . . . T-I-M-E.

Anthony P. Witham

The guys who fear becoming fathers don't understand that
fathering is not something perfect men do,
but something that perfects the man.
The end product of child raising is not
the child but the parent.

Frank Pittman

There is a place in most mothers' hearts that seeks to
protect children from harm and evil and unfairness.

Ann Kiemel Anderson

The joys of parents are secret, and so are their griefs and fears.

George Bernard Shaw

Joy of parenthood:
What grown-ups experience when the baby is finally asleep.

Anonymous

We have children because we want immortality and
this is the most reliable way of getting it

Woodrow Wyatt

I do not think my life could possibly have changed more
than it did by becoming a father.
And when my son looks up and breaks into his wonderful,
toothless smile, my eyes fill up and I know that
having him is the best thing I will ever do.

Dan Greenburg

Every word and deed of a parent
is a fiber woven into
the character of a child that
ultimately determines how
that child fits into the
fabric of society.

David Wilkerson

Your responsibility as a parent
is not as great
as you might imagine.
You need not
supply the world
with the next conqueror of disease
or major motion picture star.
If your child simply grows up
to be someone who does not use
the word "collectible" as a noun,
you can consider yourself
an unqualified success.

Fran Lebowitz

Education commences at the mother's knee,
and every word spoken within the hearing of
little children tends towards the
formation of character.

Hosea Ballou

The law of heredity is
all the undesirable traits
that come from the other parent.

Anonymous

Why not have a family motto? . . .
If the motto of a family were,
"My word is my bond," do you not think
the children of that family
would be proud to keep their word?

Laura Ingalls Wilder

Small Song for Daddy

It isn't like my daughter
to awaken at one a.m. —
but here she is.

She pulls the hairs on my chest
idly, wiggles her toes, sighs
almost as if in meditation,
and begins to sing softly,

the language hers alone,
the voice clear and fragile
as water striking stone.

New in a world where new
is all she knows, she sings
for each new wonder
as she discovers — as if those

curtains, the chair, that
box of Kleenex were created
solely to delight her.

And they do. And she sings,
not knowing she is singing
for a father much in need
of her particular song.

W. D. Ehrhart

PERMISSIONS ACKNOWLEDGMENTS

Pages 18 (bottom) and 37 (top): From *Joke Soup*, by Judy Brown. Copyright © 1998 by Judy Brown. Reprinted with permission of Andrews and McMeel publishing. All rights reserved.

Pages 20, 22, and 67: From *Enter Talking*, by Joan Rivers. Copyright © 1986 by Joan Rivers. Used by permission of Dell Publishing, a division of Random House, Inc.

Pages 23 and 25: From *Fatherhood*, by Bill Cosby. Copyright © 1986 by William H. Cosby, Jr. Used by permission of Doubleday, a division of Random House, Inc.

Page 35 (bottom): Reprinted from *And Baby Makes Three*, by Maxine Reed, © 1995. Used with permission of NTC/Contemporary Publishing Group, Inc.

Pages 40 and 42: "Homework for Annabelle," copyright 1952 by Phyllis McGinley, from *Times Three*, by Phyllis McGinley. Used by permission of Viking Penguin, a division of Penguin Putnam Inc.

Page 66: From *Poems of Childhood*, by Eugene Field. Text copyright © 1932 by Julia S. Field. Illustrations copyright © 1904 by Charles Scribner's Sons. Photographs copyright © 1996 ASaP of Holderness, New Hampshire 03245 USA. Used with permission of Atheneum Books for Young Readers, an imprint of Simon & Schuster Children's Publishing Division.

Page 75: Reprinted from *The Collected Verse of Edgar N. Guest*, by Edgar Guest. Used with permission of NTC Contemporary Publishing Group, Inc.

Pages 91, 98–99, and 100: From *Keeper of the Zoo*, by Maureen Wright. Used with permission of New Leaf Press, Inc.

Page 92: From *Life's Too Short to Live Only for the Weekends*, by Judy Gordon Morrow. Used by permission of LifeWay.

Pages 102 and 122: From *Only Angels Can Wing It*, by Liz Curtis Higgs. Used by permission of Thomas Nelson Publishers.

Page 127: "Small Song for Daddy" is reprinted from *Beautiful Wreckage: New & Selected Poems*, by W. D. Ehrhart.

GRATEFUL ACKNOWLEDGMENT TO:

Pages 30–31: Linda S. Alvarez for permission to reprint "My Baby."

Page 41: Janis Chrissikos for permission to reprint "Nursing a Toddler."

Pages 43 and 49: Judy Meggers for permission to reprint "Savana" and "Bouncing Baby Boy."

Page 48: Andre Steven Newton for permission to reprint "Jody."

Pages 52 and 107: Martha Bolton for permission to reprint her comments.

Page 73: Amy Kudro Mayberry for permission to reprint "Moments to Remember."

Page 82: Nicol Campise for permission to reprint "Beginnings."